STUDIES IN THE UNNATURAL WORLD

Studies in the Unnatural World

Keith Tuma

Wild Honey Press

Copyright © Keith Tuma, 2025

ISBN 978-1-903090-64-0

Cover photo by Diane Tuma

Wild Honey Press
16a Ballyman Road
Enniskerry
County Wicklow
A98 KX99
Ireland

www.wildhoneypress.com

i.m. Allison Tuma

"When the young people dance, they do not dance forever."

Lankum

CONTENTS

Preface   9

Oxford
Myrmecology   15
Nassology   16
Promenadology   17
Rodentology   18
Trichology   19
Ichthyology   20
Ideology   21
Escapology   22
Primatology   23
Anthology   24
Audiology   25
Musicology   26
Campanology   27
Ornithology   28
Formicology   29
Criminology   30
Meteorology   31
Garbology   32
Dendrology   33
Edaphology   34
Mycology   35

Oxford, Boston, and Malden
Thanatology   39
Cardiology   40
Demonology   41

Oncology	42
Trafficology	43
Phenology	44
Heortology	45
Pisteology	47
Eidology	48
Mastology	49
Paleontology	50
Craniology	51
Axiology	52
Eclipsazoology	54
Virology	55
Nomadology	56

Lewiston

Gerontology	59
Felinology	60
Epileptology	61
Technology	62
Toxicology	63
Teleology	65
Narratology	66

Acknowledgments   69

Author Note   71

PREFACE

The Strongman Run was one of the memorable events Diane and I witnessed in the fall of 2013 when I was in Differdange, Luxembourg to teach at Miami University's campus there for a semester and lead a study tour in Venice. A half-marathon with obstacles, the event ran participants up and down hills across the countryside and through mud and rough turf, making them climb over tires piled high and bales of hay and meshed ropes like those used in military training. At the top of one obstacle, they encountered a slide that sent them down into neck-high water, and beyond that they had to wade or swim through soap bubbles almost as deep. Diane and I had our first sight of the runners as they re-entered Differdange on Rue John F. Kennedy, the main drag in the old steel town, through lines of locals hooting their approval. It was a spectacle the likes of which we had never seen. As they passed us, the runners were coated with bubbles, and the pavement beneath them swirled with soap fumes—as if ghosts were nipping at their ankles.

That same fall, our daughter Allison was 25. She would complete her Master's in Health Administration at St. Louis University that year and begin a year-long fellowship at Children's Hospital in Cincinnati before accepting a position as a Project Manager in the Cancer Center at Massachusetts General Hospital in Boston. Allison had great friends, and many of them, and a boyfriend in a medical residency in Albany. She had everything to look forward to and she was ready for it. She was smart and witty and kind, a lover of animals including her maltipoo Moose. Allison wanted to join us in Differdange for a week, but with no space to put her up in our tiny upstairs apartment near the chateau and little time to work with because of the teaching and travel already packed into those four months, it didn't happen. She would have loved the food and sights of Paris, Strasbourg, and Bruges that Diane and I enjoyed on outings during our stay. But in the fall of 2013 who knew what lay ahead.

Allison's cancers—breast, ovarian, and thyroid—were identified in March 2017 and treated with a series of surgeries, chemotherapies, immunotherapies, and proton radiation. A year after her initial diagnosis, she was declared free of everything except the testing for recurrence she insisted on. We got on with our lives, Allison with hers. Then a couple of years later, in August 2020, I was out on our deck enjoying a martini when I received a phone call. It was Allison, with news that the cancer was back. It had spread throughout her bones, liver, and brain. Without treatment, she could have as little as three months to live.

Allison had always known that the cancer would be back and terminal at some point, and she'd say impossibly sweet things like "I hope I die first because I wouldn't want to be in the world without you." But we convinced ourselves that she'd be in her forties or fifties when she had to deal with cancer again, not 32. She'd gone through so much already, all of it seemingly endless— the appointments, the surgeries, the radiation, even the episodes of *Breaking Bad* watched and re-watched during the long recovery from chemo. It hardly seemed fair, yet here we were again.

By August 2020, of course, the pandemic was raging, and I was forced to teach remotely. The unlikely silver lining to this was that "remotely" is a relative term. So Diane and I packed our bags and headed for a rented house in Malden, Massachusetts to be near Allison as she entered her latest round of treatments. Allison too was moving, to the wharf in the North End so that her last months could be spent looking out over the ocean. As it turned out, she had three more years, initially in Boston and then up in Maine, in Portland and Lewiston. Not having toured the entirety of the European continent with Allison while I was in Luxembourg is one of a number of regrets I live with now. Allison died in late August 2023 after six years of living with cancer.

*

I started writing *Studies in the Unnatural World* before Allison's initial diagnosis. I have long been interested in the prose poem. I'm equally drawn to works that complicate the definitions of (and boundaries between) genres and disciplines, particularly when such works examine the relationship between nature and culture. I began this project with the idea of writing short works of prose or prose poetry comprising anecdote, discourse, metaphor, and speculation. These were to be organized and generated by the name of a particular discipline (I speak to friends of my "ologies"). That was the plan. Then I found myself confronted by the most "unnatural" thing I could imagine, news of a genetic mutation in Allison, our beloved daughter.

Readers might expect me to conclude this preface with a snug comparison between the sections that follow and the obstacles encountered in the Differdange Strongman event. There is nothing snug to be found here. What follows is my account of trying to accept something that I still cannot fathom. The poet John Davidson writes of how "the whited fangs of change daily devour the old demesne." I know what that means. Though it's more poetry than I need.

OXFORD

Myrmecology

The first ant of spring appears on my computer desk—she must have come over from the window looking out on the garden. She crosses a student's poem and heads for my laptop, walking back and forth across its keyboard twitching her antennae, as if unable to make up her mind. She finds the USB cord connecting the laptop to the printer, following it down toward the floor until for no reason I can imagine she turns around to come back to my desk. Pretty bold of her, I think, to be so big on entrances with no interest in exits. There's nothing for her on the desk, apparently, not a crumb, nowhere to go but back across its glass, although for all I know this is a beautiful lake in her ant's mind. Or perhaps she is thinking, "Is that all you got, Keith? Nothing else? This is your life?" She walks sideways along one edge of the desk as if gravity belonged to the human world only, then returns to the surface and reaches a stack of books I am reading. Atop the pile she comes to one about the Prado Museum featuring color images of its paintings, including my favorite, Esteban Murillo Bartolomé's *La Purísima Inmaculada Concepción*. This shows the Virgin Mary riding a shaft of gold to the heavens surrounded by cherubim, their adoring eyes looking up at her as she ascends. It belongs to a sincere genre, but I like it most for its lower right corner, where a single, precocious cherub looks away from the Virgin and out at the viewer, as if satisfied that someone is watching. It's me.

Nassology

At the library book sale I buy a few books I don't need: *Ivories of the West* by Massimo Carrà, translated by Raymond Rudorff and featuring accounts of ivory carved into "precise, premeditated shapes" using the "fine, hard ivory taken from mammoths that roamed over most of Europe," and D. H. Lawrence's *Kangaroo* with a preface by Richard Aldington, who explains that Lawrence wrote the novel in six weeks during a visit to Australia. That is less time than it will take me to read it, and I want to read it because I've always wanted to go to Australia, where my uncle has lived most of his life. I've heard quite a bit about him but met him only twice. When I was little, he brought me a stuffed kangaroo. My sisters each got a koala bear and I got the kangaroo. For a long time, we thought the fur on these stuffed animals was real. I still have mine. Its glass eyes are missing so it stares blindly out at the darkness in a basement room. The ivories are in some of the world's best museums.

Promenadology

We called him Chucky, I can't remember why—after the movie maybe. He raked leaves, cut grass in town. Had a bulldog face and aggressive gait leaning forward, working his arms with a sense of purpose. Glowered. We put his IQ at 85; we were cruel like that. Then one day we saw him pushing a baby stroller. How can he have a baby? we said. We snuck a look. He was pushing his cat around. Hmm, we said.

Rodentology

One fall I heard something moving in the wall of my study. A mouse, I thought. When the temperature drops, they come in through gaps between the siding and the dryer vent, or through a door as people come and go. The part of the basement that is beneath my study is finished so there is drywall against the original concrete wall and covering a basement window visible now only from outside the house. I like to work in my study in the evening, and that was when I first heard the mouse moving in the wall. It occurred to me that it was trapped. I started to worry that it would die in the wall for lack of food and water and I'd have to cope with the smell of it rotting. I took to spending time outside watching the window to see if I could determine its habits, and that is how I discovered that it was not a mouse but a chipmunk. It should have been easy to be rid of it by opening the window and waiting for it to scamper out, but the window was locked from the inside and I had no access to it without tearing down the drywall. I called our handyman Bill. He agreed that allowing the chipmunk to die in the wall was not a good idea. "That window has no purpose. I'll break it and we'll wait for the chipmunk to come out and then board it up." He grabbed a hammer from his van. My job was to establish when the chipmunk had left the house, and I spent the better part of two days parked adjacent on a lawn chair. Finally, the chipmunk appeared in the windowsill, following the fresh air. It sat for a minute looking out, then turned and disappeared to wherever it was living in the wall. The next evening it ventured out into the yard behind the air conditioner and ate some bird seed. What a relief, I thought, and then it ran back into the house again. I'm not going to get anything written this week, I thought.

Trichology

Is it cancer or style? She is beautiful, the bald young woman ordering yucca fries at Empanadas Aquí. I've ordered the "hairy" arepa, a shredded skirt steak with cheese in Guasacaca sauce. Diane wants the "bad girl" empanada. We're waiting for our food as the bald woman orders. We've been talking about the animals brought in for the children to see at the Latin American Festival—llamas, armadillos, and one I don't recognize. For a second I think it's a joey and grumble that it doesn't belong, and then think I'd better ask. Someone in the tent will know. "It's a Patagonian cavy," the caretaker says, "the world's third largest rodent, though I'm not an animal person. I'm a psychology major." With blue hair.

Ichthyology

"I like fish that eat other fish," the man at the next table says. "Sockeye. Not the farm-raised." The man and woman who are his dinner companions nod. "I get my hair done down the way," the woman says, and asks the older gentleman in the daffodil suit and wireframe spectacles how it went with his hip and knee replacements. "It's been two years," she says, and then, "You know me with antiques and stuff." To be sure it's a restaurant full of them, an old house. "I'm doing well," says the man in the suit, pushing up his spectacles to eyeball the label on a can of microbrew he's been delivered. I want to enter the conversation to say that farm-raised salmon are fed ground-up fish and fish waste with soy to help them grow, but I'm sure they won't appreciate the footnote—what's the big deal about free swimming anyway? If the mercury doesn't kill you the microplastics will. Besides, algae's not on the menu, and there's lots of hot sauce on my shrimp.

Ideology

Diane reads in an online community forum that there are "authentic tacos" being sold uptown, and we agree that they are worth a try for dinner with the sweet corn we've bought earlier at the farmers market. We'd noted the collection of vintage Porsches parked uptown for the annual Porsche club meeting but hadn't seen a taco truck so were curious—just how authentic could these tacos be? What would authentic even mean? At 4:30, I point the VW towards town in order to find out. Not more than three houses down South Locust I spot two young girls, middle schoolers, behind a table selling lemonade for 50 cents. How cute, I think, I haven't seen kids selling lemonade in years! The price hasn't gone up much either. Then I wonder where they got the idea and if their parents or teachers had encouraged them because they thought it would be good to teach them about business, or because the girls were restless and this was a way to get them out of the house. Then it occurs to me that this could be something more sinister. Sinister is on my mind because all day we've had news about a serial rapist found dead in his jail cell. I'm sure these girls are as innocent as Oxford permits, but I wonder as I pass if their parents have put them out in the yard on the busiest street in the city—nowhere easy to park—as ornaments. Perhaps this is something they did as children on a similarly hot day, or they'd seen it in a sentimental movie. Perhaps they think a lemonade stand is somehow American, something that belongs to another, gentler time in our nation's life that might be remembered or even reborn if we make America great again. I am not tempted to stop. Diane is boiling the sweet corn.

Escapology

I've been in the shower wondering who among the living will have a good word for me after I'm gone. A few people come to mind, but why does it matter? I'm on vacation in Rodanthe where the surf runs under a house sitting above the sand. Looking out the window I see a woman with an expensive camera filming boys and girls on boogie boards. Proximity to the water costs for owners and renters both. This house's owner has an American flag painted on a slab of wood above one staircase. It's sporting a quote mistakenly attributed to Orwell: "People sleep peacefully at night because rough men stand ready to do violence on their behalf." Okay, then, so much for my buzz. Wings up, two seagulls walk on water for a good thirty seconds before sitting down to swim. The news is all about children separated from their families and kept in cages. Everybody's transient, nobody's an immigrant in this vacation space, although I wonder about the restaurant help. At the hot dog stand I order a Pepsi and find Michael Jackson's image on the can years after he's died, his finger touching the Pepsi logo to call us to sugar and humidity, to prepare us to give up the world for a hot tub. Michelangelo's God was not so different. I think of a student's poems about growing up as an evangelical Christian, and about what his girlfriend said while dumping him. The water is wide, green up close and bluer toward the horizon. The beautiful people ride the waves way out, 300 yards from the pier in this warmer than ever world.

Primatology

The gorilla is attracting a lot of attention again. We notice that he is unkempt as zoo gorillas go, shaggy though more predictable than wild. He drools a bit, thunders his chest in what some take for comical performance and others find disconcerting, potentially threatening, etc. He squats in an awkward manner, as if defecating. In brief, he's behaving badly. We hope that, in the end, he will prove nothing to worry overmuch about. After all, he's housed in our fine zoo. Earlier we'd been to the pub to not think about our work for the zoo; we'd poured a perfect pint at the Pig & Whistle. News of the day left us alone. What the gorilla was up to was not our concern. We were surprised to see the damage to his habitat when we emerged. We know how to behave—can the gorilla not do better? Questions, and no answers. But there is always the cage. That is somewhat comforting. We have the cage to count on, we hope. It occupies a small corner of his habitat. Perhaps we'll have to put him in it, we don't know. There is not a lot of precedent. I am not a book, another gorilla said, many years ago. This gorilla can't read.

Anthology

A friend from Tennessee says they're called assets, these mostly wrecked machines that gradually take over the tiny yard of our neighbor around the corner halfway down the block. A rusty red pickup truck is up on blocks at the curb in front of the house, with no engine or exhaust pipe, bald tractor tires piled in its bed. It seems unlikely that it will ever move again, but it got to the house somehow. An only slightly newer red pickup is in the driveway with its hood off, its owner peering into its engine. Behind this pickup, there's a silver sedan, and in the middle of the yard a PT Cruiser. Lawnmowers and snowblowers and wheelbarrows are out of the garage and crowding the porch with stools and tables and various gadgets. There's a mini-tractor that my neighbor uses to pull a wagon to offer his adorable little girls rides around the block, as if life was a carnival, or maybe a petting zoo. Toys and boots and bikes and the other property of these daughters are scattered everywhere. Out back their dog barks as I pass with one of our dogs. His daughters smile and wave. I've known a few hoarders, mostly hoarders of papers and books, but it's not the custom in these parts to park that many machines in one's yard. It's easy to imagine the nearest neighbors upset about their property values. "He's not one of us," I imagine them saying. "He's from someplace else, maybe Tennessee." Long ago I put together an anthology of poems by poets who live elsewhere. I know the kinds of things that are said about such gatherings.

Audiology

At dinner with the visiting translators I hear about the girlfriend of the poetry translator and her commitment to rescuing animals—a dog missing its front legs and soon to be fitted for a cart, a feral Italian kitten smuggled into the country via Montreal, a dozen parrots. Parrots often outlive their humans, the poetry translator says, and his girlfriend's adopted birds speak the history of their city. One pipes up with "Juanita!" and coughs forcefully, as if to remember a marriage ended by emphysema, or a crotchety old man yelling for his nurse. Another says "I need a drink" and "Turn on the ice machine." Another sings "Jiggle the handle," suggesting the location of its cage in its former life. And so on—expressions of intimacy and love compete with curses to map the range of human emotions among deceased parrot lovers. Some parrots parrot other birds, so the house is a conference of birds, the poetry translator says. One evening he had an edible and endured the mimicry for hours in that altered state. The other translators laugh at the thought. They have told their stories about the trials of translation to an assembled student audience; their work is done. Now among peers and hosts they are freer in their speech. "Never tell a story that good to a fiction writer," the translator of fiction says to the translator of poetry. Twelve parrots and an edible.

Musicology

"Are we going to play or pose?" the legend asks. Ever sideways as a front man, reluctant to give straight answers to dumb questions, he's angry at the crowd. He'd rather not be photographed. He wants to be playing music, and who can blame him? He's played so long. If he stumbles backwards over a monitor while berating his audience nobody thinks he could break a hip, though there's little that's Chaplinesque about him anymore. He plays a lot of the Great American Songbook as if it's soon to be *his* book, songs for music lessons and old timer shows of interest mostly to scholars. I don't recognize this one, some say of his own songs, or worse, they do and don't like them played that way. He knows there's nothing deader than last year's beat. He plays, and while some like it more want to be able to say that they were there to hear him play. So he poses, but only for so long. Soon he will be with the other legends—Monk percussive and sparse, offbeat; Jerry with the baroque arpeggios and Jimi with the matchbook at Monterey; Aretha and Marvin who could melt an audience in any key—and the not so famous too, exploded stars already almost forgotten: Cherry Wainer with the popcorn eyes, Lefty Dizz bending the blues on the slide. Love me love me not fade away. Right.

Campanology

The door is wide open, and there's no leaving. The company is such; the obligations that brought us linger. They will be heard. Ding dong. There's no leaving, and the door is wide open. These are recorded bells, a carillon playing commercial pop, avoiding religious songs. Still, we are hailed by the sound, summoned to "Jingle Bell Rock": the door is wide open and there's no leaving. Snow won't muffle what cold air carries outdoors between classes. The blabbering trees and whispering grass are in their winter. They don't need to know. We do, apparently. Ding dong. The door is wide open, and there's no leaving.

Ornithology

A sparrow built her nest atop our porch light three years in a row. The porch is not enclosed, so she easily came and went, making a twiggy mess of our all-weather rug. We watched her fly away every time we left the house. No matter how often we saw her zip to a branch on the other side of the driveway, we were pleased, surprised again and again. She watched us make our way to the garage and then returned to her nest. Our comings and goings must have been a nuisance for her, but she came back every spring. We had no idea what she did when we switched on the porch light. Did we cook her eggs? So far as I know there were no nestlings. One December I took down her work but learned nothing. We waited for her and then took her for granted. We were only so good at keeping an eye on her. But she gladdened three summers.

Formicology

Not everyone knows that as a young man St. Francis of Assisi was a party animal. Even after the Perugians held him in a dungeon for a year he liked the good life. It wasn't until after he joined the Crusades that he began to turn his life around. The first step was returning home to ridicule. After that, his conversion experience was a long one. Preaching to the birds and so on—that was years later. These ants from my yard didn't have that kind of time to work with, alas. Theirs was a short life. The hummingbird feeder was badly designed, a dish with six holes allowing multiple hummingbirds to sit and suck. The holes are big enough for little ants to climb down into the sauce, simple sugars making for a sticky situation. They devoured its contents in an hour.

Criminology

Is criminology a sub-discipline of physical anthropology or a branch of psychology? I'd rather study painting. There are more photographs of criminals than paintings, however, especially if one counts mug shots. Mug is slang for face. If you mug me that's a crime, but mugging for the camera is not. Add portraits of politicians and we even the score a little. We are all sinners, the Bible says. Some get over it. Some get away with it. Stick figures are all I'm good for when I draw.

Meteorology

Gabi Roach, *Deep Clean*

Her head is a galaxy out of proportion to her body, its roundness at odds with rectangles that structure the drawing. Or it is a lollipop on the stick that her neck is. Either way, she is faceless while doing laundry, deep cleaning with an old-fashioned washboard, hands in the sink, an apron protecting her dress. Multiple male faces press close against the laundry room's windows watching her work. In the window on the right the biggest of them sports a snout, grinning halfway to leering. Above him as if standing on another man's head is a leprechaun with one outsized hand waving at her. But she has turned away. In the middle window smaller faces are stacked like rocks in a narrow glass. One appears to be in pain. Another wears a condescending frown. On the left, a face that could be Charles Baudelaire's looks away from the scene. It's like a busy day at the zoo—such crowds and then finally! "The poor thing—she's not so different from the other hippos now that she's grown up." After four days of rain, better weather.

Garbology

On the same day I find two dead squirrels under the lily of the valley in the garden, my sister tells me she's taking advantage of trash amnesty week in our late father's city to empty his garage. Much of what she's throwing out doesn't surprise—rusty tools and nails, a cooler full of old cat food, income tax returns going back to the 1950s. But she's also tossing the Incredible Edibles machine from our childhood. I'd forgotten it. You put rubbery goo in a mold and heat it to make gummy sweets: Luscious Lizards, Tasty Turtles, Beetles Brittle. There was also a mummified possum under Dad's workbench, she says. There were always wild animals in his yard, and after Mom died he was too generous to them. If a skunk or a raccoon wanted to come in via the cat door to eat with the neighborhood cats, fine. Goodbye, Dad.

Dendrology

It's a mush of melting snow in the backyard under the trees. I'm waiting for the little dog Moose to smell what he wants to smell and do his business, as some call it. He's lost in discovery. Our two white pines, twins almost, and the oak and tulip tree loom tall and ancient, older than the house, older than me. It's dark and quiet and I have nothing that needs doing, though I want Moose to be done so I can get out of the cold. After a week of sub-zero temperatures, branches litter the ground, waiting for a warmer day to be gathered and tossed into the woodpile I've established among the honeysuckle that forms a natural border at the back of the lot, hiding the stone building that once was the farmhouse for this land. A natural border, we say, as if there were such a thing. We mean anything other than a fence. As Moose noses around I happen to look up in time to see a black branch falling from the tulip tree. These trees aren't only old, I think, they're falling apart. It's dangerous to be under them. The branch hits the thawing turf with a thud. Then I see that it's not a branch but a less than athletic squirrel. That's a first, I think. I'm too old to believe in a natural world, but it's harder to give up on talent. It takes the squirrel a second to regroup and run back to the tree.

Edaphology

Verbascum thaspus, a.k.a common mullein, a.k.a Indian ragweed, a.k.a cowboy toilet paper—as soft as lamb's ear, its leaves—prefers disturbed dirt, the stony soil one finds alongside railroad tracks or at the edge of industrial parks and other wastelands. Also called Adam's flannel and beggar's blanket, this monster with its tall spikes of sulfurous flowers stalks our garden. I look out my study window at twin towers flanking the air conditioning unit, one plant bent around the shepherd's crook. Two more of the monsters live around front, one of them growing through the leaves of our Japanese maple. Mullein in tea is an expectorant, and that's not all it's good for—it treats earaches and warts, even hemorrhoids. In Europe, it's associated with witches, its dead leaves like a skirt pushing out below the waist. In Roman times women used it to make dyes to color their hair, and Aristotle knew about its narcotic effect. It's easier to catch fish where you see mullein beside the stream, he wrote, since fish swim more slowly when stoned, like most of us. Quaker women are forbidden makeup, but mullein rubbed on cheeks causes an allergic reaction that reddens them— we're never so clever as when we need to get around prohibitions. Our neighbors say they're weeds, but they are more impressive than what we've worked so hard to keep alive—zinnias, lantana and hibiscus, hollyhocks and marigolds. Miracle-Gro helps them all, but I never need it for the mullein. Only the little weed with leaves like a Christmas tree, also an interloper, competes with the mullein to hold our attention. Its purple is blue-black like a bruise.

Mycology

for Nik Money

For some problems, there is no solution, not now nor in the future, while for others we can find a way to make things better. My neighbor doesn't like the deer who have made his backyard, and ours, their own, eating flowers and vegetables, leaving copious droppings even the dogs pass over for a choice cat turd. A mob, he calls them, not incorrectly. We could pressure the city to reduce the deer population or act more locally by doing away with our compost pile. All of that might stop him from thinking he is doing something useful by tossing his baseball bat at the deer to chase them from his yard into ours. My friend the mycologist is not that comical, but he's good for irony, noting once as part of a lecture on fungi that everything we need to decompose us is already present in our stomachs. No composting needed. More recently, he has been worried about climate change. He fears there's no hope for us with the warming that is ahead and all that follows from it. Even if we can pull down all of the CO_2, he says, the damage has already been done. But if there is no hope for us, there is this: the end of the human race will mean the end of suffering. Or so he says. I had to think about that since I grew up in a religion that has human suffering at its core. What about the cockroaches that survive us? Won't they suffer when we're gone? And what about, God forbid, the deer?

Oxford, Boston, and Malden

Thanatology

After the trumpet vine grew to the top of the utility pole, its red flowers rising thirty feet, it turned to a nearby pine tree. Distracted by other matters, I didn't know it had designs on the pine until I spotted a few flowers high up in the tree. Upon further examination I found a vine half as thick as a wrestler's thigh coming out of the ground under the tree. This can't be good for the pine, I thought, and fetched my saw. I hoped that after I killed that part of the vine the pine would recover, but my opinion of the trumpet vine had changed and I began thinking about how to be rid of all of it. The crew that trims trees to keep them out of power lines was in town, so I contacted them. The company's representative came by but declined to take down the vine, by this point wrapped around the pole in tangled layers. "It will only grow back," the man said. "Not if I keep hacking at it with an axe every time it pokes out of the ground," I replied. "Or I will poison it." But he didn't return. So I paid my neighbor with the landscaping business to chop it down. I worried about him cutting around electric wires without experience with this kind of work or a cherry-picker to lift him, so I told him not to cut in and above the wires. This left six feet of dead vine at the top of the pole. "Gravity will take care of it," I told him. Seven years later most of it hangs on, the twiggy wig of a witch. The pine tree it murdered has been removed.

Cardiology

I knew my heart was broken before the CT scan with calcium scoring turned up scary numbers that sent me to the cardiologist. I'll be seeing him for the rest of my life. Tom Raworth has lost his life, but my news reminded me of his heart problems. Tom was one of the first open heart surgery patients in England. He was given to playing with his medicines to try to counter his high blood pressure. Not always strictly following doctor's orders, he sometimes self-medicated, or he did until they found his colon cancer. During a break at the Cork poetry conference a few years earlier, Trevor Joyce drove Tom, Diane, and me out to Ballymaloe. Touring the gardens we came upon a bed of poppies not quite in bloom. Tom pulled out his Swiss Army Knife and cut off a bud to taste its milk. When my cardiologist recommended the Mediterranean diet and I began reading about foods I should be eating, I came upon stories about the ghost pepper, until recently the hottest chili pepper in the world. Tom was proud of the ghost pepper plant he grew at his apartment in Brighton, and back in the day I thought this had to do with his fondness for hot sauces and spicy foods. Now I suspect that it may also have had to do with the anti-inflammatory effects of capsaicin in the arteries. How do you mend a broken heart? You burn a hole in your stomach.

Demonology

There's a cow on the roof eating grass. Or maybe that's another movie where everything is upside down, and not *A Town Called Bastard*, *A Town Called Hell* for the American release. Telly Savalas plays the bastard, a small-town tyrant with a crooked smile, bald and sweaty as one should be in hell. Stella Stevens arrives in a coffin, accompanied by her faithful servant, who may be deaf. He is wicked with his gun. She is looking to avenge her dead husband. The town's priest is a retired Mexican revolutionary; he's the one who murdered her husband. The priest dies in the movie and the tyrant too. Lots of people do. Some places obviously haunted by the dead are tourist attractions. Pripyat with its Ferris wheel, for example, is in the news again as the shelling continues. Haw Par Villa in Singapore is another, though the Buddhist demons there aren't real, like the dolls of Nagoro set up to remember everyone who left town. They're scary, but not like shelling is. The skeletons in the Capuchin Catacombs are real, and you can tour those too. Go to hell, why don't you. The new barbarism is like the old barbarism, except for the nuclear weapons.

Oncology

The oncology nurse likes to talk about everyday life—traffic this morning during her commute to the city, plans for a holiday still a few months away, her daughter's decision to quit college and move in with friends in a tiny North End apartment. "And who is paying for that?" The oncology nurse is friendly, but this is her professional talk. She's killing time for Allison, who is waiting for chemotherapy. The drugs must be made up and bagged on the morning of the infusions. Pharmacists must wait on white blood cell counts to get the go-ahead. The oncology nurse acts as if she has all the time in the world. I have come from far away, Allison's boyfriend too. We've driven across town to buy dry ice to freeze the blue turban Allison will wrap around her head to keep her hair from falling out. "Would you like some crackers?" the oncology nurse asks. "This first one will take forty minutes," she says, and names the drug. Allison knows its name already. "The steroids will keep you strong, more energetic than usual, for a day or two." The oncology nurse reminds Allison that she'll need to flush her toilet twice if others are staying in her apartment. If she has a high fever she is to come back to the hospital. She's seen the blue turban before, yes.

Trafficology

Odd to spot a white SUV parked in the middle of the open fields of the nature preserve, between soybeans and the woods. As Dora and I approach we see a Bernese Mountain Dog in the backseat and its driver walking in circles, eyes fixed on the grass in the way one walks while looking for something. "Do you need some help?" I ask. "That's okay," he says, "I usually bring two bags, but I only had one today and he's pooped twice. I went back to get a bag, but I can't find his poop." It's a big field, and with all the dogs and other animals that roam it no doubt it includes plenty of droppings. "I'll look a little more," he says, and then, as I am walking away, "I apologize to the universe." In the last five years Allison has lived with three cancers. Several good friends have passed away much too soon while another is living with stage four colon cancer. There's no need to apologize to the universe.

Phenology

For a few days the blossoms of the pink peony are bigger than my fist, nearly half as large as my head. Soon after, the flower droops towards the stone path, where the careless might trample it. It's too beautiful for its own good, too sumptuous. That's the truth from Keith to Keats; cut it for a vase. There's more support in shrubs, in families though not in mine. We have only the one plant beside the garage, and only one daughter, also dying. Who would want to read a miserable poem about that? Maybe the gods would if I ask nicely, or if I cry out. The gods love best those who die young, but what do they know? Some say Peony is from Paeon, who died when his teacher Asclepius thought he had become too beautiful. Zeus turned him into a flower to save him from the consequences of that observation. Good job, Zeus.

Heortology

All Saints Way is on Battery Street off Hanover in Boston's North End, a gated alleyway crowded with images and memorabilia celebrating Catholic saints. I'd never seen it at Christmas so was pleased to see it lit up as I walked from Allison's apartment on the wharf to pick up a pizza we'd ordered from Rina's. The pizza there reminds me of pizza we've had in Italy, where Allison will never visit. She's been to lots of places, though, and has taken to repeating what her lawyer boyfriend from Lewiston likes to say about family being more important than travel. With the news of her terminal illness, we came to town at the end of August, and one of the first things we did was go to All Saints Way, which Diane hadn't seen. We walked around checking out the restaurants that had moved out into the street and a few tourist sites—an old graveyard where Allison and I posed for Diane to photograph us. It was like we were on vacation, although Diane fought back tears when I asked her to pose with Allison in front of the gate at All Saints Way. The North End hosts St. Anthony's Feast in late August, but the pandemic made that impossible. We would have just missed it anyway. No doubt it resembles festivals throughout the USA with ethnic food and activities for kids and bad music played by brass bands. It's been happening in the North End for 100 years after being brought over from Montefalcione. I'm not Catholic, but I ought to appreciate St. Anthony for his bookishness, as represented by El Greco, among other painters. Like a poet, he preached to odd audiences—to fish, most famously. His tongue was magical enough to be granted relic status. There's also a story about a mule and the Eucharist, and plenty of kitschy images fit for All Saints Way. But I'm over it when it comes to being a snob about painting. Charles Dickens thought John Everett Millais's painting of the juvenile Christ in Joseph's workshop with Mary and her mother Saint Anne made Mary look like an alcoholic in "the lowest gin-house in England." Today it's part of the collection at Tate Britain. I can't remember if Allison and I saw it the year we visited museums in London and left our umbrella on a boat after half an hour on the Thames. Later, we were thoroughly soaked running down Tottenham Court Road in the rain, headed for an Afghan restaurant where the food, like the company, was miraculous.

Pisteology

"Man's accidents are God's purposes," Sophia Hawthorne wrote, scratching it into a window in the study at Old Manse, the Emerson family home in Concord. It's the highlight of the tour, or it was when Diane and I visited the house on our honeymoon. Reading about the house, I see that I'd forgotten she'd used her diamond ring to do the damage—Sophia, that is. I must have seen the little pane of old glass minutes before I fainted. Nurse Diane said I had low blood sugar after an exhausting drive up from Newport, but would it matter if I said I was seized by a ghost and tossed to the floor? We are in New England again, the land of dead writers, where Allison has had that same fainting problem among others far worse. She loves it here, but I am questioning God's purposes. When her terminal diagnosis prompted a move to the wharf, I helped her empty her apartment at Whittier Place, a high-rise near Mass General, where Allison works and also is treated. The crew that came to take away the couch had never read Whittier's *Snowbound*, I'm certain, and neither have I. It isn't half bad as narrative verse, some say. Trevor says his poems are blocks of wood to bite down on to hold off his pain; Bob von Hallberg says he can find no way to accommodate ours. Unread but immortal, Whittier is also a bridge near the New Hampshire border. We drive across it to buy Diane's menthol cigarettes, which are illegal in Massachusetts. Thoreau's name is everywhere too, like bad habits. His walkway outside Whittier Place leads to the hospital. Once I thought it was funny to stretch out on Emerson's grave to be photographed. Now I read more closely: "I dilate and conspire with the morning wind."

Eidology

At the RusMoloko farm, cows are given VR goggles to make their winter summer and improve their milk. Grass is harder to fake, though not impossible. It took me two months before I realized that the patch of it no larger than a gravesite in front of an old house in Malden was artificial turf. I thought life might just be a little greener in Massachusetts. Allison's illness has all of my attention, but there is this question too: why install a tiny rectangle of artificial turf for your front yard? It's not much of a job of mowing that is being avoided. It must have been about having a patch of green forever bright against the crumbling asphalt everywhere in Malden. In a documentary about near-death experience, similarly unreal colors swirling on screen are used to represent a disembodied perspective. "Visualize the bat hitting the ball," my father said, when teaching me to play baseball, but I never became a slugger. All glove, they said. I don't take advice well, but I like to give it: hay soaked in beer broth is a favorite among lactating cows after the meadow no longer feeds them. Or, as Baudelaire said, get drunk!

Mastology

Not two minutes after we set out the half mannequin on Lebanon Street a young woman pulls up to put it in the back seat of her Honda. "Oh my god, it's brand new!" In the northern suburbs of Boston there's always something at the curb. The half mannequin had been Allison's, who used it to advertise clothes online. Having disposed of the clothes she no longer needed while moving to an apartment on the wharf, she wanted to be rid of the dress form too. It was difficult not to consider its buxom shape beside the reason for its removal: Allison's metastatic breast cancer diagnosis. After her double mastectomy two years earlier, I spent a few weeks with her in a rental house in New Hampshire. Her Beacon Hill place was off limits after the upstairs tenant's washing machine flooded both his and her apartment. I asked the other man upstairs for His help when I first heard about Allison's cancer, before I knew that it was not one cancer but three, a trinity of cancers. I prayed that she be allowed something like a normal life, but there is no such thing. In the 1940s and 1950s, American companies sanded the nipples off their mannequins. Allison was proud that her surgeon had pioneered the surgery that preserved hers.

Paleontology

My father's cat was KT, a big orange tabby found on a horse farm in the Bluegrass state and sweet as a cat can be in the neighborhood. I thought his name was a tribute to initials I share with my sisters, but it was a mistaken abbreviation for the state. It certainly didn't refer to the KT boundary separating the age of reptiles from the age of mammals, although I feel that far away sometimes, ready for a meteor or a giant asteroid. There's no comfort at all in knowing that Allison's death will be one of 42,000 breast cancer deaths happening every year. Cancer is a replication error; there are too many mistakes. The sky is clear blue this morning. Nothing is headed this way.

Craniology

One midwinter morning a beach ball appears in the backyard of our rental, as if dropped from the heavens to interrupt the purgatorial rhythms of lockdown. We watch it roll toward the trash left by previous tenants—sticks and bricks mostly, but also a queen-sized bed frame through which a scraggly sapling grows. It's easy to get rid of things north of Boston, but the bed frame offers us something to talk about—until the beach ball arrives. It is the fifth month of our daughter's treatment for metastatic breast cancer. Trump has started an insurrection, and more than 400,000 Americans are dead in the pandemic. Did the teenager next door decide the beach ball wasn't worth retrieving? Is this somebody's idea of irony after a snow storm? My head hurts. Wind tosses it from tree to tree.

Axiology

You don't know who you are. You don't know what to do. You want to go home because you are more comfortable there than you are in your rental house. Your house in Oxford is modest, but you are used to it. Your books are there, your music. Your rental house is serviceable and allows you to visit your terminally ill daughter nearly every day, but it is old and dusty, its siding dirty pink, its wallpaper turning yellow, except in the stairwell where it presents a scene of country life even though the house is on the busiest street in Malden, a gritty working-class Boston suburb. Its washing machine sits beside the kitchen sink and doubles as a countertop. Everything you cook in its kitchen tastes the same, like mold, your wife says. Chicken tikka masala like mold, chicken pot pie, chicken wings. Your clothes slowly turn to rags because there is a pandemic, and in your hurry to get to Boston following the news of your daughter's illness you were only able to bring so many of them. You order new socks and T-shirts and wear them over and over and wash them in the kitchen, dry them in a basement half concrete and half stone, damp and damper. You spare your wife possible injury by lugging cardboard boxes of wet clothes up and down stairs, ducking your head to avoid the low ceiling. Your wife cries nearly every day about what she knows is coming. You cry sometimes too, though privately in the interstices of work you feel lucky to have. Your wife is also ill and often unhappy, sometimes violently so. One day she throws coffee in your face because she thinks you are telling her what to do. Another day she picks up a fire extinguisher and threatens to crash it through the door of your makeshift study. She rants about the house and what you are doing in it. Facebook returns memories for her every day, but her own short-term memory is compromised. You want to go home where you suspect she will do better, but you know that it will never be the same to live there. It makes you sick to your stomach to want to go home. You wonder if it would be a good idea to go home for a short stay to know that you have a life in another house and not have one house be associated with living and the other with dying, but you are afraid that while you are away something awful will happen to your daughter. You want to be with her at the end, and when you are able to think about it you realize that both houses will be associated with death from now on. You have no future. Galen Strawson tells you that you have no future in his book of essays, which you are reading: *Things That Bother Me: Death, Freedom, the Self, Etc.* Going home is part of etcetera, a bothersome illusion. You want to go home but fear that wanting to go home is a form of betrayal. You want to go home and you no longer have a home.

Eclipsazoology

Odd to notice the pink feet of the mourning dove on the roof of the porch below my window in the house in Malden. It's the last day of March; there's nowhere I want to go on the day before I'm to be vaccinated. With my mother and father dead, some of my best friends gone, and Allison terminally ill, what's the point of going on? Yet I don't want the virus. Yesterday Diane and I drove up to Plum Island with the dogs to meet Allison and Dan at the Sandy Point State Reservation. After touring the salt marsh, we drove down a gravel section of road to the beach on the southern end of the island. We didn't know that dogs are not permitted on the beach there and were taken aback when a man in a neck gaiter told us. He wouldn't report us, he said, but he wanted to be sure we knew. He was worried about the piping plovers that return every year to nest on the beach. I thought of the horseshoe crabs I saw swarming the shores of Cape Cod when I was a boy, their population devastated now because their blood is useful to medical research. I remembered a day decades later when I drunkenly pissed on a statue commemorating the carrier pigeon in a Wisconsin park. It's hard to remember too much of the world before Allison was in it. Because she thought dogs were allowed on the beach until the end of March, skinny Allison in her headscarf told the big man in the neck gaiter to fuck off. We didn't see a single piping plover.

Virology

> Philip Guston, *The Coat II*

Among the upper crust in old Hangzhou it was customary to brew seven varieties of tea at the beginning of summer, a different tea for the three houses on one's right, three more for the houses to the left, and the last for the household. Tea was served in porcelain bowls—enough for a single sip. The closest I've come to this community-building ritual is passing a joint. You don't take an extra hit without being called out for bogarting. That was forever ago, though, before community was community-spread. No doubt the tea ritual is toast now too. Are we forever to become shells of our former selves? If so, this painting should grace our flag—in the foreground, an empty buttoned-up coat standing on blood-red turf, more than a little tired, holding matching pants and shoes. All else recedes into robin's-egg blue.

Nomadology

After we've been eight months in Malden, Allison has a brain MRI indicating no disease progression and we decide to go home to take care of doctor and dentist appointments. It's early spring, colder than expected. Arriving at the house, I see in moonlight the peach tree Diane's friend Pascale gave us when she was dying of cancer. It's in bloom but otherwise looking the worse for wear. Long ago, deer amputated half of it, so it grew sideways rather than up. When it finally topples over, the squirrels will miss the golf ball-sized peaches they carry off annually, an entire tree's worth in one night, with Amazon-like efficiency. Under the full moon I see the turf chimneys from which the cicadas will emerge after waiting 17 years to sing to one another and die. No backups for 633 days, my computer tells me. Easily fixed. I wonder if my father's gravesite is still covered with the straw the cemetery staff put down in September. I remember the rhododendrons in bloom another time we visited my mother's gravesite before he joined her, and the rhododendrons in bloom when a pregnant Diane and I spent an afternoon feeding ducks and coots in the gardens beside Reed College. There were rhododendrons all over Malden too. "You have to watch them or they grow into trees," an old man said when I praised his while walking by one day.

Lewiston

Gerontology

We left for Lewiston in early June, allowing enough time to make two stops and still make it there ahead of Allison's 35th birthday on June 9. We stopped to see my sisters in northern Ohio and then at The Turkey Hill Inn in Bloomsburg, PA, familiar to us from our trips to the East Coast during the pandemic. That inn was the only good thing about those long drives—I'd send Allison a photo of my dirty gin martini from the little bar there after too many hours on the road. Because Diane also was ill and felt like her problems were being put on the back burner, she wasn't thrilled about making the long drive east again. Allison didn't want to hear it, however, when I tried to defend her mother's views about this or most matters or pointed out that not everyone was as strong as she was. It had been six years since her initial diagnosis, and almost three years since she called me with news of her terminal diagnosis. At one point during her first set of surgeries and treatments, she gave me Atul Gawande's *Being Mortal*, saying "I think you'll like this." Gawande notes that in the Roman Empire the average life expectancy was 28 years. His book describes "the story of our parts" as we age, trying to understand aging "not so much as a natural process as an unnatural one." The Tang Dynasty poet Tu Fu has a less prosaic take on our decrepitude: "The body grows weaker, but gazing at the mountains remains the same." But six years of living with Allison's illness did plenty to change the ways I look at things too. My sense of humor is not what it was. My tastes in music and literature have shifted, though not in every case. Roger Grenier's *The Difficulty of Being a Dog* remains important to me: "And what if literature were a dog tagging along beside you … that hurts you by dying before you do, short as a book's life is, these days?" Though Diane's problems with her short-term memory were getting worse, I said to our neighbor, "We're going up to Maine for the end" and packed up the car. The dogs, at least, were ready.

Felinology

The cats of Capernaum walk between columns of the excavated synagogue. In another photograph, an orange tabby peers into a tourist's backpack in front of the Church of Saint John the Baptist in Ein Karem. This could be one of the websites Allison scrolled through while resting in bed in Lewiston near the end. She grew up with Chloe—only one in five orange cats is female, she liked to remind me. Rescued from a dog's mouth as a feral kitten, Chloe would dig her claws into my chest while kneading my shirt. She spent her last months in our basement, dragging herself with her front legs, soiling herself. "You are selfish to keep her alive," Allison said, and one day looking into Chloe's eyes I knew that was true, though she tried to climb out of the box on the way to the vet. She'd moved into the basement to stay away from Moose, who later came along with us to Lewiston as we set up in Allison's basement, a few weeks before she went into hospice care two floors above. We put up a gate to keep the dogs from going upstairs, though they made their way there eventually.

Lee, the ten-year-old orange tabby Allison adopted from a shelter six months before she died, spent his time on or under her bed. Up or down, on or under, he wasn't going anywhere, and neither was she. I read to her to give her something to do other than scrolling—chapters from Prince Harry's memoir, the whole of Maurice Scully's *Humming*, the "Pride of Cats" from Jan Morris's *A Venetian Bestiary*. The vagabond cats that once were everywhere in Venice have since been moved out of the sestieri most popular with tourists. Stone lions mean nothing without them.

Epileptology

Her pineapple salt lamp needed batteries, and Allison was trying to order them online. She decorated her condo with pineapple candlestick holders and pineapple artwork, even a pineapple blanket. Pineapples are welcoming, she'd say. Sir Thomas Browne wrote about the "rhomboidall protuberances in Pineapples maintaining this Quincuncial order unto each other," but Allison's boyfriend, the fifth in his family named John and called Five, wondered if something was off when he looked at the website and saw she was about to order 300 batteries. Right after he left for the gym, her seizure started, her speech incomprehensible. She got up to wander with an elsewhere look in her eyes. Diane and I helped her to the stairs, turned her around and lifted her one step at a time. "Reverse rump-bump," the nurse called it. In her bedroom, there was suddenly lucid speech, but from a voice that belonged to someone else: "You are afraid," she said, our eyes meeting.
"I *want* to die." Then it was back to speaking in tongues; she remembered nothing afterward. In *Mark 10* Christ casts out the demon, which follows other anecdotes about transfiguration and the voice of God speaking from the clouds. Few believe these are more than stories. Caught up in the madness at Loudun centuries later Jeanne des Anges was told her body housed seven demons, one of them lodged in her forehead. Allison's brain mets were "little ants," she'd say, thinking of the way they showed up on the MRIs, lesions throughout her brain, the most dangerous of them in her brain stem. The test of demoniacs was the ability to converse in a foreign language unknown to them. Allison used plain English.

Technology

Allison and I left at 5 a.m. to be on time for her appointment at Mass General, trying to miss the traffic that chokes the road north of the city. She'd had her brain MRI the previous week but didn't see the report online. The delay had something to do with the Fourth of July, she thought. Either that or they wanted to give her the bad news in person. She was taking her second trial drug. At the Yawkey Outpatient Center, she completed the usual preliminaries—urinating into a cup—and we were led to a corner office to wait for the Nurse Practitioner administering the trial. She was eight months pregnant and all smiles. Allison sat on the paper spread across the examination table and I took the chair beside the desk. The nurse put her tiny flip phone on the desk and said the brain oncologist would call. It looked as out of proportion as the giant mobile phone James Garner's character holds to his ear in *Barbarians at the Gate*. Soon we had the news thanks to it. The drug had failed. It would be hospice. I asked about trying the miracle drug Enhertu again, but no, there were no viable options. Allison was quiet. The doctor apologized twice for not being there, and then it was time to go. The nurse wished us well: "It's good to see you again!" On the way back Allison wanted to listen to *Love in the Time of Cholera*, her favorite book, but I talked over it about the day she was born. Her car seat fit best in the passenger seat of our Renault, so she rode home from the hospital in Portland, Oregon beside me. "We've done this a lot," I said, "from Portland to Portland. Now you get to be older than me." She had the same smile. Then we talked about where to stop for lunch.

Toxicology

One September Allison and I were turning left on a country highway when a man in a truck pulling a camper van rear-ended us—time stopped for a minute until I thought to get out of the car and check the damage. When I unbuckled my seatbelt, Allison was already out of the car and on the phone calling for help. I didn't notice that the collision had thrown her wig and glasses onto the dashboard. I'd managed to stop our SUV on the side of the road we had turned onto, its bumper ruined and its back window blown out. This was Pleasantville Road, just a mile from the family reunion we were now late for. Family was not our strength, but we knew this might be our last chance to see relatives on my mother's side. Diane didn't want to come because she and Allison weren't on the best terms, and six hours on the road for a two-hour event was too much. When Allison first learned she had breast cancer, she consulted every doctor she could about her options and without hesitating elected to have a double mastectomy. Diane said she should consider a lumpectomy so as not to disfigure herself. A history of simmering mother-daughter conflict reached a moment of crisis on another of Allison's solo trips back to Oxford when I had to step between them to break up a fistfight after Allison pitched an acorn squash at Diane when she said something too familiar about her being spoiled. After that, communication between them was often limited, other than complaining about one another to me. But there was always love between them, despite appearances. I knew that. After she lost her speech in her final week, Allison would occasionally pick at something invisible in the air in front of her as she rested, as if drawing out fine threads, fine loose threads. Then one day Allison lifted her arms toward Diane as if trying to hug her. But Diane was looking at something else in the room. A few days later, about an hour before Allison died, Diane arrived in the bedroom. She started manipulating Allison's legs as if to get her up and moving somehow, the actions of a primal mother, I thought, more than those of the nurse she had been long ago. I saw up close then what the hospice nurse meant when he said that near the end the dying body shuts down its extremities to preserve its inner core.

Teleology

All summer it rained, a heavy rain that ran over the gutters and coated the windows of the Lewiston condo. In what is usually a dry August, it was an advertisement for global warming. Nobody wanted to be out in it, but one early morning while walking the dogs I thought I saw my first minks, two of them squealing far out of the Maine woods, chasing one another into puddles. With all of that water, seal-coating the condo's parking lot took forever, and the rain couldn't beat back the poisonous fumes, as if the cancer that was killing Allison wasn't enough. Like everybody else, the hospice nurses had to park on the street up the hill, and what was promised to be two days turned out to be five before the contractors painted the lines. The parking lot wasn't in bad shape, and I could imagine no purpose other than aesthetic for such disruption, but it wasn't my decision. It was the condo board's call. I knew they didn't like me, the man with Ohio plates. One day the director of the board told me not to allow my dogs to do their business in the grass behind the mailboxes. "It's a new rule," he said. "I'm not living here long term," I replied. "My daughter is dying upstairs." That ended our conversation. I should have told him, "The end is where we start from." We watched as one thing after another was taken away from Allison: her balance, her speech, and then, after three days of breathing wet and ragged, breath itself. But for a minute or two before she died all was calm and I was able to pray for her and say goodbye. I saw her surprise at who or what had arrived to meet her just for a second before her head rolled to the side.

Narratology

At the Oxford Kroger, I run into Don, the father of one of Allison's friends from long ago. He's been working out, he says, trying to recover lost muscle mass: "Long Covid," he explains. "I'm regaining the weight, but it's all flab." I give him the news about Allison but assure him that I don't worry about her. The night before Allison died, I tell him, I asked her to send me a sign, afterward, to let me know she is okay. The only original thing about a desperate father saying that was my adding, "And please don't be too subtle about it." I'm used to people raising their eyebrows when they hear talk about such matters, and to eyes looking discreetly away. But there are also people who feel compelled to share their hopeful stories. The Episcopal priest around the corner told me about driving past a field full of Caterpillar heavy machinery on his way home from his father's funeral, the morning sun shining on brand new farm equipment. His father had been a salesman for the company, and the sight brought him to tears—adult tears, he said, which are different from the tears of children. My story is the same at least as far as the tears are concerned. On the first stop on that long final drive home from Lewiston, something odd happened to Diane at the Hyatt outside New Haven. We'd had breakfast downstairs and I was loading up the car, going back and forth to the room, anxious to get on the road. Diane said, "I'm having this strange feeling, a buzzing in my head, like I've left something." I hurried back to the breakfast room, and there was her purse on a chair beside our table. Many hours later, exhausted from the second day of driving, I saw that the exit for Bloomsburg was just a few miles off. I was glad to have a bed waiting at the Turkey Hill Inn to recover for the last leg home to Oxford. And then there it was, a truck directly in front of us with a big sign reading ALLISON in bright orange letters. We followed the truck past the Bloomsburg exit so Diane could photograph it. It was headed to Indianapolis, the home of

Allison Transmission, as I learned later. We followed it for a few miles until we were sure we had the photograph and then took the exit to turn back to the inn as I watched it pull around a car on its way west.

Acknowledgments

Some of this writing has appeared, sometimes in a different form or with different titles, in *Chicago Review*, *Coast/No Coast*, *Datableedzine*, *The Laurel Review*, *Silver Pinion*, *Poetics for the More-Than-Human-World: An Anthology of Poetry and Commentary*, and in *Dos poetas norteamericanos* (Elaine Fowler Palencia and Keith Tuma), an English/Spanish edition of selected poems translated by María Auxiliadora Álvarez, Michael Palencia-Roth and Linde M. Brocato with introductions by María Auxiliadora Álvarez (UANL 2024). My thanks to the editors, translators, and publishers.

The line attributed to Tu Fu in "Gerontology" is from Eliot Weinberger's excellent "fictional autobiography" of the poet, *The Life of Tu Fu* (New Directions, 2024).

Thanks to Rich Housh for writing music for and recording "Musicology" for the June 16, 2023 episode of *The Watt from Pedro Show* podcast: https://podcasts.apple.com/us/podcast/2023-06-16-the-watt-from-pedro-show/id79745987?i=1000617311827

Thanks to Randolph Healy, Jacquelyn Mitchard, Hugh Sheehy, Catherine Wagner, and especially William Walsh for their extraordinary feedback on manuscript drafts. Thanks to Alice O'Brien for help with the cover image.

Thanks to María Auxiliadora Álvarez, Alen Amini, Jody Bates, Ann Belknap, Kathy Bernstein, Brad Blackstone, Martha Blackstone, Lee Ann Brown, Mairéad Byrne, Julie Celantano, Dan Cepela, Susan Chabot, cris cheek, John Clifford V, Roger Conover, Mary Jean Corbett, Owen Joyce-Coughlan, Madelyn Detloff, Graeme Doran, Erin Edwards, Ellen Elder, Karen France, Fergal Gaynor, Priyadarshini Oshin Gogoi, Eric Goodman, Jim Heynen, Daisy Hernandez, Zackary Hill, Bing Hinton, Trevor Joyce, Deanna Katko, Justin Katko, Frances Kruk, Matt Kunkleman, Alice Ladrick, Steven Paul Lansky, David Lloyd, Jonathan Lohr, Margaret Luongo, Peter Manson, Lee Martin, TaraShea Nesbit, Hoa Nguyen, Vincent Palozzi, David Schloss, Tom Schmidlin,

Dustin Simpson, Billy Simms, Kay Sloan, Eirik Steinoff, Amy Toland, Sam Toland, David Toms, Michael Ureneck, Laura Van Prooyen, Robert von Hallberg, Vernon Williams, Saleh Yousef, and more students, former students, colleagues, doctors, nurses, friends, and departed friends than I have room to name here for support of all kinds during the years I was writing this book.

Thanks to Dr. Arvind Ravi (MD, PhD) whose knowledge and wisdom Allison often benefited from. I excerpt here from his description of Allison's genetic mutations in an email to me, quoted with his permission: "Genetic testing for Allison assessed 8 commonly mutated genes in hereditary breast cancer, including the well-known BRCA1 and BRCA2 genes. Her testing detected a CHEK2 mutation. CHEK2 is a critical mediator of DNA damage response, essentially 'raising the alarm' that there may be mutations that require repair and helping activate the appropriate downstream repair (or cell death) cascade. Her particular mutation, I157T, has been associated with multiple cancer types including breast historically, as well as more recently granulosa cell tumors of the ovary, which is one of the rare tumors that Allison had. In addition to germline testing, she had tumor-tissue specific testing (a.k.a., somatic testing) looking for alterations specific to the genomic makeup of her cancer. Testing of her breast tumor showed three additional variants:

PIK3CA E545K
NF1 frameshift insertion/truncation
ERBB2 (HER2) copy number gain

PIK3CA acts as a component of one of the main growth factors signaling cascades of the cell, becoming activated when cells are in a 'resource high' setting to produce intermediate messengers that go on to promote proliferation and survival. The E545K mutation leads the protein to have increased activity, essentially hallucinating a kind of 'green light' with respect to the abundance of growth factors in the environment even when that may not be the case; hence their role in the unrestrained proliferation that is a hallmark of cancer."

Author Note

Keith Tuma is the author of books including a volume of selected poems, *Climbing into the Orchestra* (The Mute Canary, 2017), *On Leave: A Book of Anecdotes* (Salt, 2011), *The Paris Hilton* (Critical Documents, 2008), and *Fishing by Obstinate Isles: Modern and Postmodern British Poetry and American Readers* (Northwestern UP, 1998) and the editor of books including *Anthology of Twentieth Century British and Irish Poetry* (Oxford UP, 2001) and *Rainbow Darkness: An Anthology of African American Poetry* (Miami University Press, 2005). He lives in Oxford, Ohio.

www.ingramcontent.com/pod-product-compliance
Lightning Source LLC
Chambersburg PA
CBHW060342080526
44584CB00013B/881